CLAPHAM

ERIC SMITH

published by
THE CLAPHAM SOCIETY

COVER
Return from the Derby, Clapham Common, by J. P. Herring, engraved in 1862. The scene, which is set on South Side close to the present-day junction with Elms Road. The Windmill Inn can be seen in the background.

The Bandstand on Clapham Common shortly after its re-erection on the Common in 1890. It was one of a pair which were designed by Captain Francis Fowke and first erected in 1861 in the Royal Horticultural Society's gardens in South Kensington.

© *The Clapham Society*

Hon. Treasurer, Charles Williams
40 Shandon Road, London SW4 9HR
All rights reserved
Printed in Great Britain by
Battley Brothers Limited
37 Old Town, Clapham, London SW4 0JN

ISBN 09500694 26

CONTENTS

INTRODUCTION

This is a picture-book of Clapham. Emphasis is on early drawings, water-colours and photographs, and on prints, portraits, or plans not easily available elsewhere. It was first published in 1976 by the London Borough of Lambeth and now appears in a completely revised format and with some additional material.

Eric Smith, the author, was for 50 years between 1937 and 1987 Hon. Secretary and Archivist of the Clapham Antiquarian Society. He amassed a large collection of books and papers and undertook research into Clapham's past, and this book reflects some of the fruits of his labours. Eric died earlier this year and it is perhaps fitting that the book should now re-appear. Before his death, Eric had assisted with corrections and revisions to the text. The book remains very much his work.

The text remains largely as in the 1976 edition. It is intentionally brief, the aim being to provide the reader with an introduction to the history of the Clapham area of south London.

Clapham in mediaeval times was a small village on a hilltop overlooking the Thames, and the truth of this statement is easily established by anyone standing in the old churchyard today. It remained a village, to a great extent, until after the Napoleonic War when a period of expansion began. It is true that the destruction of the City in the Great Fire of 1666

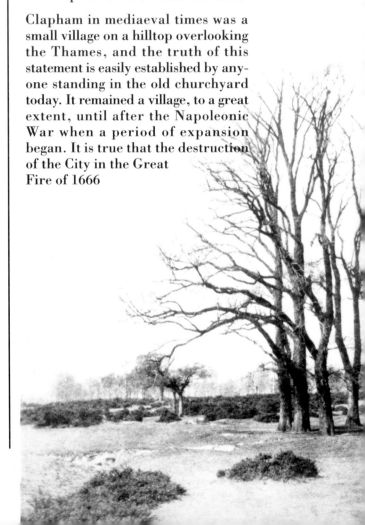

drove many people to seek new houses in nearby places, and that some of these came to Clapham and probably did not return. And it is certain that slowly throughout the eighteenth century large houses belonging to City bankers and merchants were built around Clapham Common, but it was not until well into the nineteenth century that the parish began to take on the aspect of a suburb. The change was accentuated by the development of Clapham Park by Thomas Cubitt, and even more by the coming of the railways. In the 1850s, the first of the large estates began to be developed, and from that time onwards, slowly but surely with ever-increasing momentum, the Clapham we know began to take shape.

NICHOLAS LONG

ACKNOWLEDGEMENTS

The Clapham Society wishes to thank Frank Phillips for designing this new edition, Nicholas Long for editing and making additions to the text, Elizabeth Long and Patricia Long for assistance with editing and typing and, not least, the members who made the loans which made publication possible.

The Society also wishes to thank the London Borough of Lambeth for permitting the re-publication of the book.

Picture credits; page 95

THE FIRST PARISH CHURCH

The two drawings dated 1754 in the Minet library are the oldest representations that we have of the old parish church of Clapham. The drawings are neither good nor accurate, but they do give a general idea of the appearance of the building which previously stood on the site of the present St Paul's Church, Rectory Grove.

No description of the mediaeval church survives. Some time in the sixteenth century a chapel was built to the north of the chancel and this was later used as a burial place by the Atkins family, the lords of the manor. In 1650 Sir Denis Gauden built a north aisle in continuation of the chapel and in 1653 Walter Frost added a chapel at the south-eastern corner over the grave of his father. In 1710 this too was extended westwards, providing a new south aisle. In 1717 the north aisle was rebuilt with a vestry room at the west end.

From this it will appear that very little of antiquity was visible externally when the sketches of 1754 were made. Fig 2 shows the porch at the western end, and over the roof gable of the nave, a curious erection (possibly a bell turret) surmounted by a weather vane. Fig 3 shows a north-east view with the blocked window of the Atkins Chapel clearly visible, and the eighteenth-century vestry room projecting from the north aisle. Except for those in the Atkins Chapel, all the windows appear to be eighteenth century.

By 1774 the parish church was in poor condition and no longer conveniently sited for its increased congregation. It was therefore agreed by Act of Parliament to build a new church on a corner of Clapham Common.

This remaining portion of the old Holy Trinity Church is shown in two drawings by a local artist, Bartholomew Howlett, which are bound up in a magnificently illustrated copy of Manning and Bray's *History of Surrey* (extended from three volumes to 36 and now in the British Museum). The drawings are in sepia wash and give a very attractive view of the building and some of the congregation in the early nineteenth century.

2. Pen and ink sketch of Clapham Church in 1754
3. Pen and ink sketch of Clapham Church in 1754

The interior view shows the two brasses on the south wall, and some other memorials now gone. Opposite, between the windows, is the fine monument to William Hewer, in whose house Samuel Pepys died in 1703. Hewer was an Admiralty official and a large landowner in Clapham, who died in 1715. A portrait-bust of him in an oval is supported by two cherubs, and it can still be seen in St Paul's Church, where it has been most beautifully cleaned and restored. Portions of the Atkins monument remain as well as a small fragment of the Clerke memorial which is shown here on the end wall just above the head of a lady visitor. There are eighteenth-century box-pews and a tiled floor. The stairs must have led up to a west gallery.

Bartholomew Howlett, the artist, was born in Louth in 1767 and came early to London as an apprentice to the engraver James Heath. In 1811 he was married and living at 6 Brewhouse Buildings, a row of cottages which adjoins the brewery in the Wandsworth Road, probably at no.

4. *North aisle of Old Parish Church*
5. *Interior view of Old Parish Church, drawings by Bartholomew Howlett, c.1800*

6. St. Paul's Chapel, by Bartholomew Howlett, 1816

522 (now part of a public house). In 1817 he issued the first and only part of a projected Topographical Account of Clapham, which was to be drawn and engraved by him. It was to have six numbers with three plates in each, with letterpress 'from the most authentic sources' which would not only cover the topography of the parish but would also contain biographical notices of persons resident in, or interred at Clapham. An engraving by Howlett showing the east end of the north aisle immediately prior to its demolition appeared in the *Gentleman's Magazine* for December 1815, together with a very good account of the memorials and other features. The illustration gives an attractive glimpse of the village beyond the churchyard.

The present church was completed in 1815, and was a typical Georgian 'preaching box' built as cheaply as possible in stock brick as a chapel of ease to the new Holy Trinity to accommodate the inhabitants of the new streets which were being built in the eastern part of the parish which until then had been farmland. The architect was Christopher Edmonds, and the cost £5,000.

HOLY TRINITY

7. *Clapham Parish Church, lithograph by C. J. Greenwood, c.1850*

The new church of Holy Trinity was built in 1774-76 on a piece of ground donated by Mrs Penelope Pitt, the last of the Atkins family. The architect appointed to build the church was Kenton Couse (1721-1790). The site stood high but was not otherwise very satisfactory, as there was continual trouble with the foundations during the succeeding century. The ground was fenced round and the perimeter planted with elms to take the place of those felled to make way for the building, and the last of these remained standing until as recently as 1953. In 1807 a wrought-iron railing was erected in place of the wooden one which had been painted olive green and had done service for 30 years. This and the elm trees can be seen in the accompanying lithograph by C. J. Greenwood of about 1850. The railings went for salvage during the last war, but were replaced by Lambeth Council in 1988. The clock in the turret is the original one supplied by Mr Thwaytes of Clerkenwell for £144, and four bells by Thomas Janaway hang above it.

Just at the rear of the church was a group of small cottages known as the Polygon, and built in 1792. The inhabitants were in the habit of hanging their washing to dry on the Common, and the new church fence was soon put to such undesirable use. Hence the order made on 6 September 1777 'That the Beadle be directed if he finds any cloaths hanging on the Church Fence to throw them off'. Another of the beadle's tasks was to direct the coach traffic on Sunday mornings. The original portico was enlarged in 1812 in order to allow members of the congregation to alight more comfortably when it was raining, and in the days when Venn was rector it became necessary to appoint a second beadle to help regulate the traffic. When the church was filled to overflowing chairs were even placed in the vestry at the east end to accommodate extra people, so great was the crowd that came to hear the preacher.

The interior of the building has changed little except for the addition of a new chancel and Lady Chapel in 1903. There are galleries still on three sides, but the box-pews were cut down in 1875 and the benches in the centre for those who could not afford to rent a pew have long since gone. The three-decker pulpit, which had a handsome sounding-board, has been reduced in size but is still in use. The east end as arranged for the opening on 10 June 1776 must have been very splendid. It included a wooden reredos with 'the paintings of Moses and Aaron from the old Church if they shall be found worth putting up', a communion table covered with crimson velvet, more crimson velvet hangings for the pulpit and desk, and a gold-fringed crimson curtain draped above the painted glass in the window. The interior was modernized in 1875 and in 1903 the church was extended eastwards by Beresford Pite (1861-1934). At this time the original reredos was retained and moved back to its present position, but the glass by William Peckitt of York, which had fascinated Lord Macaulay in his boyhood, disappeared when the stonework of the window was moved to the south side of the new Lady Chapel. The fine communion table went into the vestry, from which it has only recently emerged; and a new organ by a local firm, Hunter and Son of High Street, was placed in the chancel. At some period the carved Royal Arms of 1776 vanished from the church, and in 1875 a new font was installed. One order of the vestry in 1776 is perhaps worth quoting: 'That no curtains be put on the tops of pews, nor no hatpin be fix'd in the pillars, nor no holes made in the tops of the pews to stick Christmas in'.

In the library of RIBA are two very interesting drawings of the interior of Holy Trinity Church in 1842, when

8. Holy Trinity Church interior in 1845

8

9

9. *Children's Galleries, erected 1842 in Holy Trinity Church*

extra galleries were erected for the children of the parish schools. The architect for the alterations was J. B. Papworth (1775-1847), who had also worked at St Paul's Chapel, and the illustration above shows the new galleries, which were supported on iron columns in the shape of palm trees. They were taken down in 1914, but the archways cut in the end wall to make way for the necessary entrances remain.

The organ in the west gallery was installed in 1794-95, but it does not appear to have been an exceptionally good one, and in 1844 a 'new interior' was supplied by Mr Bishop for £635, with an allowance of £150 for the old one. This remained in use until 1903, when the Hunter organ was installed in the chancel. The old case, which was a decorative feature, remained until it was badly damaged by blast during the last war. Surmounting it may be seen the Royal Arms of George III, given by a Mr Vials in 1776. All the interior woodwork was of oak, and the windows were of plain glass with the exception of that at the east end.

10. Holy Trinity Church, lithograph by C. J. Greenwood, c.1850

OTHER CHURCHES

ST MARY'S, CLAPHAM PARK ROAD

This is an architect's drawing of the Roman Catholic church of St Mary in Clapham Park Road (or Acre Lane as it then was) designed by William Wardell (1823-1900) and built in 1851. Next door is the large Georgian mansion, once the home of Samuel Thornton and of Lord Teignmouth, which by this time had been divided into two residences. One was occupied by a Mr Soltau and the other by a doctor, Sir William Pearson, who sold his part to the Redemptorists. The church was completed; the day of consecration came, and the peal of six splendid bells rang out joyfully. But Mr Soltau, whose bedroom was only a few feet from the belfry, did not like it and obtained an injunction. The bells were silenced until his death in 1864. Then the Redemptorists bought the house and the bells pealed out once more. Since that day the church has been twice enlarged and two more bells added to the peal. In 1892 the old house was pulled down, and John Francis Bentley designed a new north transept for the church and also the red-brick monastery adjoining it. In the forecourt is a war memorial cross designed by Sir Giles Gilbert Scott.

11

12

13

11. *St. Mary's Church, 1857*
12. *Interior of St. James's Chapel, Park Hill, 1829*
13. *St. James's, 1845, water-colour by E. Duncan*

ST JAMES'S, CLAPHAM PARK

In 1828 a new gothic chapel was erected in Park Hill by voluntary subscription and consecrated in 1829. The architect was Lewis Vulliamy (1791-1871) who lived at no. 53 South Side. As may be seen from the little water-colour by E. Duncan, 1845, its surroundings were then quite rural. The church was enlarged in 1870 and a tower built.

The building was bombed in 1940, and a number of interesting memorials perished with it. The new church was designed by N. F. Cachemaille-Day and was opened in 1958.

CLAPHAM RECTORY

It is not known when the original rectory was built. A note written by a local builder in 1811 calls it 'a very antient building, the newest part having been built a century ago'. At this time it was in poor condition and required a considerable sum to render it 'a thoroughly commodious and respectable residence for the Rector of so opulent a Parish as Clapham'. Money was found, and the alterations produced the 'plain' parsonage shown here in a water-colour of 1827 by E. Hassell (at present in the Battersea Library). At the time of these alter-

ations John Venn was the incumbent, but not for long as he died in 1813. He was succeeded by the popular and persuasive preacher William Dealtry. When Dealtry died in 1847, the Lord of the Manor, William Henry Wentworth Atkins Bowyer, became the new rector. He only lived in the house for a few years however, before commissioning a new rectory in Macaulay Road. The old rectory was pulled down and the site built over in 1880.

Of the earlier rectors we know little,

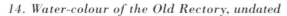

14. Water-colour of the Old Rectory, undated

14

15

but in March 1601 Edward Couchman was instituted and came with his wife and three children to live in Clapham. In the autumn of 1603 there was a serious outbreak of plague, and 21 people died in the parish. The first to be struck down on 3 September was the rector, followed by his wife on the 4th, his three children during the succeeding fortnight and his maid on the 24th.

In 1706 an Irishman, Nicholas Brady, arrived at the rectory. His main claim to fame is that in 1696 he published a metrical version of the Psalms, which he had compiled in conjunction with the Poet Laureate, Nahum Tate, and which for nearly a century was usually bound up with the Book of

15. Water-colour of Clapham Parsonage by Hassell, 1827

Common Prayer. It was familiarly referred to as 'Tate and Brady'. Anthony Blackwell, headmaster of Market Bosworth Grammar School succeeded in 1726, resigning in 1729 to make way for John Goodwin, Rector of Market Bosworth, who remained at Clapham until his death in 1753. Then followed the long incumbency of the absentee Sir J. Stonhouse, who held the post for 39 years, during which period the house was let, only returning to its proper use on the arrival of John Venn in 1792.

THE MANOR HOUSE

Our view below of the Manor House of Clapham, which stood close to the old parish church, is by W. F. Zincke, 1796. It is a view looking down Rectory Grove towards the present church and the turret, with its little cupola that was later to provide the name Turret Grove, can clearly be seen. There had been a house there since at least the fifteenth century when it was occupied by the Gower family, but this was rebuilt in the reign of Queen Elizabeth I by Bartholomew Clerke, Dean of the Arches and Member of Parliament for Bramber. He came here in 1580, and in 1583 he entertained Queen Elizabeth, a fact only known because of a brief entry in the Lambeth churchwarden's accounts: 'Item, for ringing ye Queenes majestie when she dined at Clappam and went to Grenwitche iijs.iiijd.' This was a great honour, but was also liable to be a great expense, and in 1594, when the house was about to pass into the hands of Henry Maynard, Secretary to Lord Burleigh, rumour that the Queen proposed to pay another visit there scared off the would-be purchaser. In 1616 it was bought by Dr Henry Atkins, physician to King James I, and it remained in the hands of that family for some two centuries, though they seem to have seldom lived there for any great length of time. In 1624 it was leased to Sir Robert Heath; in the 1640s it was occupied by Sir Robert Needham; and finally, in 1749, it ceased to be a private residence and it became a school.

16

17

16. The Old Manor House, a drawing of W. F. Zincke, 1796

17. View of the Manor House, by J. C. Buckler, 1823

The second drawing of the Manor House by J. C. Buckler in 1823 shows the cupola had gone. The only contemporary description that has survived was published in 1804: 'This edifice which is situate near the old church is now a ladies' boarding school. Some coats of arms in one of the rooms having been destroyed a few years ago it cannot now be ascertained by whom it was built. Both from the external structure and from the pannels and chimney pieces in the rooms, it appears to be of as old a date as Queen Elizabeth. An octagonal tower the base of which forms a bay window in a large room now used as the school rises somewhat higher than the rest of the house and terminated in a dome, makes a very singular appearance.' The park of 15 acres extended to the Wandsworth Road, then called the Portsmouth Road, and included six fish-ponds.

In 1749 Mrs Margaret Castelfranc opened a boarding-school for young ladies there. She was not married, but in the fashion of the day adopted the more dignified title to distinguish her from the much younger Misses in her care. She was of Huguenot descent, born in Ireland in 1720, the youngest of a family of eight. The school obtained a good reputation, and was the largest of many such establishments in Clapham. The school survived until about 1830 after which the house was used for a few years as a boys' school under Dr Laing. It was finally demolished in 1837, and Turret Grove and its flanking terraces cover the site.

MATRIMONY PLACE

A path through the old churchyard of St Paul's and down a series of flights of steps led to Matrimony Place, adjoining the Wandsworth Road and a favourite spot for local artists in the nineteenth century. In this picturesque corner Charles Floris and his wife Emily, of 7 Fitzwilliam Road, painted a cheerful wedding scene in 1896. 'The work tells its own story,' they wrote in their advertisement, 'and the dramatis personae have been drawn from actual residents in the locality'. A pencilled note gave a clue to the identities of the main figures. In the background was the vicar, the Reverend Herbert Hughes, standing with the parish clerk, Mr Collins. On the steps was a Mrs Goodrich, of Fitzwilliam Road. The bride was a Miss Hetty Warren and the groom Mr John Mielboom, also of Fitzwilliam Road; Ernest Kirk was the boy in the right-hand corner, and Ernest Jones in the procession waved to the girl in the upper window. Sadly, the event was fictitious, even though the people shown were local residents and to that extent authentic, the Parish Register revealing that a Mr Mielboom never married a Miss Warren.

18

18. Matrimony Place, 1955
19. Matrimony Place, by C. L. Floris, 1896

The picture sold well at a guinea a time as a mezzotint photogravure. Emily, the co-artist, went on to design stained glass for Messrs Powell of Whitefriars and to paint china for Minton's.

19

ALFRED HOUSE

Alfred House stood opposite the old rectory in what is now Rectory Grove, a more recent name for a road which has been variously known as 'the Street', 'Church Lane' and 'Larkhall Lane'. It was one of a number of large old houses which stood in this area of which only one, Thurston House, now remains. For many years Alfred House was a private school kept by the vestry clerk, Mr William Franks, and it was pulled down soon after these two water-colours were painted (the first by Sophia Colson, the second by H. Hopley White in 1855). It can be glimpsed through the window of the octagonal schoolhouse in B. Howlett's engraving. Next door, where Fitzwilliam Road now runs was The Firs, the home of Captain Robert Hudson, master of an East Indiaman, who died there in 1817 leaving a fortune of over £90,000. A painting of this house was shown at an exhibition in 1928, but unfortunately its present whereabouts is not known.

20. Alfred House, water-colour by Sophia Colson, 1855

21. Alfred House, water-colour by H. Hopley White, 1856

Further along Rectory Grove on the same side and almost opposite the church is a house called Cromwell Lodge which, though the house and façade were altered in 1925 (by Stanley Hamp of Messrs Colcutt & Hamp) for a Mr Barry Neame, is of considerable age. The name of the house recalls an unsubstantiated tradition that Oliver Cromwell once lived in the village. Some old drawings of the Manor House are indeed entitled 'Cromwell House', and Cromwell Cottages are nearby. The Atkins family were certainly supporters of Parliament in the Civil War, and it is possible that Cromwell may have stayed hereabouts for a short period.

21

OLD TOWN

Old Town, formerly 'the Street' or 'Clapham Street', was, as the older name implies, the main thoroughfare of the village, which, in its earliest days, led down from the main London road, curving eastward through the fields past the parish church and on to Lambeth, with a branch road leading off by the schoolhouse down to the Portsmouth Road. Even today it retains an old-world atmosphere, and our pictures show two of the older groups of buildings that survive.

The houses, nos. 39, 41 and 43 Old Town, are referred to in a document of 1707 as three new brick houses recently erected by Daniel Clarke, citizen and Merchant Taylor, and although neglected for many years they were restored some years ago. No record remains of their earlier occupants. Nos. 39 and 41 have both in their day been used as private schools and doctors' surgeries, but it is no. 43 that has had the most interesting inhabitants. From 1844 to 1862

22. 39-43 Old Town, 1913

22

it was tenanted by the Reverend James Hill, Minister of the adjacent Congregational Church, and it was during his ministry that they gave up their eighteenth-century chapel, the gabled front of which can just be seen in the accompanying photograph (taken in 1913), and moved to a fine new gothic building in Grafton Square. From 1876 to 1896 the architect John Francis Bentley lived in the house, as indicated by an LCC blue plaque on the front wall. He had practised as an architect in the Adelphi for some years, and in 1874 had married. After a short honeymoon he brought his wife to live at Clapham in furnished lodgings in Belmont Road, and then, in January 1876, they moved into no. 43. Here he stripped off innumerable coats of paint, and in some cases wallpaper, from the panelling, and to the drawing-room he added a rear-extension with a large four-light window. He designed his own dining-room furniture in oak with the motto 'Be Merry and Wise' across the back of the sideboard, and on one of the doors he painted a pot of marguerites (his wife's name was Margaret). Here too he installed his collection of blue and white Oriental china and Venetian glass. His greatest work was the

Roman Catholic Cathedral at Westminster, the tall tower of which can be seen on a clear day from the roadway outside the house, and he also made additions to the church of St Mary in Clapham Park Road where he was a regular worshipper. By 1894 there were nine children in the house, and it was decided to move to no. 3, The Sweep, where he died in 1902. The next tenant was M. H. Lapidge, nephew of the architect Edward Lapidge. He was a clever artist, and illustrated many medical books and papers with microscopic drawings that were much in demand. He also acquired a wide knowledge of prints and engravings of all kinds, especially Japanese prints, of which he had a large collection and on which he lectured. He was also a keen sportsman, member of a rifle volunteer corps, and is described as a clever, good-looking, and well-loved man with a great sense of humour. He moved to 69 Bromfelde Road in 1903 and finally left the area six years later. In 1915 Russell George Alexander came to reside at no. 43. He was a foreign news-editor of the *News Chronicle*, a poet and an artist of some distinction, and a great friend of the artist and engraver F. L. Griggs. He remained until 1938.

THE POLYGON

The Polygon was built in 1792 as recorded on a tablet destroyed by bombing in the 1939-45 War, but there were almost certainly previous buildings on that site. The grocer's in the photograph (1949) has a splendid old shop-front, very little altered. In 1855 it belonged to Charles Wingate, a grocer who also indulged in building speculation and constructed Chatham Road across the grounds of one of the Five Houses, which until then had stood in splendid isolation in Bolingbroke Grove, Wandsworth Common.

OLD TOWN

The picture postcard reproduced below provides a view of Old Town in about 1925: a nostalgic scene with little traffic apart from the car in the background and two buses waiting to set off. The bus nearer the camera is on route 42 which went as far as Finsbury Park Station. The horse trough just behind the buses has been moved to the entrance of Grafton Square. The fire-station is in the distance and the house in the centre of the picture was demolished when Maritime House was erected in 1939, the shop, a barber's, too, is gone.

23

24

NORTH STREET

North Street is one of the older streets in the area, and the photograph shows a block of eighteenth-century houses, North Row, awaiting demolition in about 1900. It was formerly known as Nag's Head Lane.

25

23. The Polygon, 1949
24. Old Town, c.1925
25. North Street, 1900

26

CLAPHAM FIRE BRIGADE

26. New Fire Engine House,
Old Town, 1869

The Clapham Fire Brigade was described by a local newspaper in 1868 as 'useless', and in the same issue appeared an engraving of a patent steam fire-engine manufactured expressly for Hewitt's Brewery fire-brigade in Larkhall Lane. It was felt, however, that people should not have to rely on a private firm for aid in case of fire, and so in the same year the old watch house was conveyed to the Metropolitan Board of Works for conversion to a fire-station. The watch house was in fact pulled down, and a new fire-engine house erected on the site in 1869. One man lived on the premises, but the rest of the firemen, and the horses, were lodged elsewhere. The new building, seen in the photograph, has since been converted into a residence. The object to the left of the picture is the new fire escape, a canvas chute which was tried out in 1862 with small boys 'at Mr Harvey's in the Terrace, Mr Deane's on The Pavement, the Misses Elliotsons and the Rectory'.

THE CLAPHAM PAROCHIAL SCHOOL

The school at Clapham stands on a corner site in the Old Town where the road forks, and the date when it originated is not precisely known. In a deed of 1648 (the year which the school itself takes as its foundation date) the then Lord of the Manor, Sir Richard Atkins, granted to the inhabitants of Clapham for ever the school house and the land on which it stood, and he refers to it as the school 'which they or some other Benefactors had built at their own cost and charges'; but when is not stated. The deed also appointed a number of trustees, and this was the cause of much trouble about half a century later when an argument arose as to whether the trustees or the inhabitants should appoint a schoolmaster. The argument was acrimonious. Both sides made an appointment, and one group padlocked the schoolhouse door, whereupon their opponents sent for a blacksmith and broke it open. Finally, in 1700, there was a lawsuit. We do not know the outcome, but a bundle of affidavits have survived which provide much interesting information.

The first question which each witness was asked was, 'Do you know the publick Grammar School house in Clapham?' and this suggests that in its earliest days it was a school of some standing. This is borne out by the fact that one of its masters, Dr Samuel Pratt, later became Dean of Rochester, and that Samuel Edgeley, Vicar of Wandsworth, sent his son there in preparation for Eton. The 'three Rs', Latin and Greek were taught, as well as 'accompts' and we learn from Read's *Weekly Journal*, 27 December 1735, that at Christmas a Latin play was performed. 'Last week', it says, 'the scholars educated at the Grammar School in Clapham performed one of Terence's Comedies before a polite audience which honoured the young Performers with their Presence. The just manner of their speaking and acting was the admiration of all the spectators.' About fifty years later, nevertheless, it became a free school or charity school, finally evolving into the parochial schools, with girls and infants in the Old Town and boys in the new building erected in 1838 in what is now Macaulay Road.

The two illustrations over page show the school as it was in about 1812. The exterior view is a water-colour in the British Museum, and portrays the octagonal school, built by voluntary

27

subscriptions in 1809, and gives it a much more rural appearance than it in fact had. The engraving is an internal view of the same school, 'conducted on the system of the Madras School invented by Andrew Bell DD', and once again is the work of Bartholomew Howlett. Through the windows are fascinating glimpses of the street outside, now called Rectory Grove. Dr Bell's system was based on pupil-teachers, and here we can see in the one schoolroom at least six classes being taught by the eldest or brightest boy in each group, while the master and his assistant sit in splendid isolation in a small alcove at the rear. The infants in the foreground on the right are playing at a sand-table such as can still be seen in the village church at Dennington, in Suffolk. There was further rebuilding in 1850, and the octagonal school was replaced in 1887 by the one which now remains and which has only quite recently been given up. The quill pen weather-vane, and the oldest of the several foundation-stones have been transferred to the new Macaulay School which in 1974 was completed in Victoria Rise.

27. Water-colour of Clapham Free School as rebuilt in 1809

28. Internal view of Clapham School by Bartholomew Howlett, 1812

28

29

CHURCH BUILDINGS

The row of Georgian houses, built in 1720, was known first as The Buildings, or The New Buildings. They became Church Buildings with the advent of the new Holy Trinity in 1776. A keystone in what was, before a disastrous fire in 1955, an arched entrance beneath the first floor of no. 14, gives the date of the building as 1720, the initials of the owner I.H.S, and the date when the leases

30

31

would expire, 1913. A lease in the Greater London Record Office tells us that on 10 January 1714 Miles Corbett of Old Brentford leased to John Hutt, Senior, of Southwark, carpenter, for 199 years Burnt House Close on which Hutt was to erect good and substantial houses within seven years. He built, and no doubt designed, twelve in all, nos. 12-23 North Side, and of these ten survive. John Hutt died at Clapham, in 1738. On the expiry of the lease in 1913 the terrace was purchased by the Westminster Hospital as the site for its new hospital. The threat of demolition hung over the buildings for 20 years; in the event only nos. 22 and 23 were demolished in 1934, and flats built on the site ('Okeover Manor' and 'Woodlands'). Nos. 15-17 were gutted and made into a single set of flats in 1935, to the designs of David Robertson, No. 12 was much altered and its front wall rebuilt in about 1950.

The photograph, figure 33, taken in about 1930 shows no. 13 and part of no. 12. The former, known

29. Hollyhurst, 13 North Side
30. Keystone to arch, 14 North Side
31. Crest and shield in overthrow of gate, 13 North Side

32

now as Wren House and formerly Hollyhurst, is undoubtedly the finest house in the row still in single private occupation. It has the original iron railings and after heavy blast damage from nearby bombs has been well restored. Certain modifications were made in 1935 mainly to the rear façade and including the reconstruction of a bow-window of about 1830 to the left of the front door; but these have not spoilt the symmetry of the building. Not long after the house was built it was tenanted by a John Bullock, one of the Bullocks of Faulkebourne Hall, Essex, and it was no doubt he who put up the shield with the family crest of a helmet sur-

mounted by five battle-axes tied with a red cord (see photograph). It may be that the arms were once painted on the shield, but it is now blank. John Bullock died in 1740, and after the death of his daughter Rachel, it passed to some cousins named Cracherode, a name which local rate collectors found difficult and which was on one occasion entered as Scratchlow. The most important member of that family to reside here was a very wealthy bachelor, the Reverend Clayton Mordaunt Cracherode, whose magnificent collections of early printed books, prints and coins are now in the British Museum. In 1802 the house was leased by Francis Garratt, a City tea- and coffee-merchant whose son became the Lord Mayor in 1824. He was followed by his daughter Eliza, by then married to the Reverend M. M. Preston who in all probability added the two bay-windows to modernise his residence. After being a surgery and a girls' school, it reverted once more to private occupation, and at the time of the 1897 Jubilee a local paper refers to 'the dazzling splendour of Mr Miller's private residence, no. 13 North Side'. At the time of the 1935 Jubilee a floodlit Union Jack flew from the parapet.

33

34

35

32. *Church Buildings, North Side, c.1920*

33. *Woodlands, North Side, c.1920*

34. *Archway Place, formerly at 21 North Side*

35. *Stabling in Archway Place, at rear of North Side, c.1920*

No. 14 North Side was the home of the novelist Graham Greene for a short period before the Second World War. His book *The End of the Affair* is set in Clapham during the War.

THE ELMS

The site of the Trinity Hospice is one of the most interesting in Clapham as here stood what may well have been the most splendid mansion in the Parish, but of which no picture has yet been found. It was built in 1663 by a City businessman named Sir Denis Gauden, and in the same year Samuel Pepys notes in his diary that he visited him there. He admired the house and the gardens and described the visit, the first of several, in some detail. The house was later bought by William Hewer, who greatly improved it, and here Samuel Pepys came in 1700 when ill health necessitated his leaving London to seek the purer country air of Clapham. 'Your Paradisian Clapham' as his friend and fellow-diarist John Evelyn described it. Pepys died there in 1703, and Hewer in 1715. The old house remained until 1754, and the only description we have of it is that 'it formed three sides of a square, the principal front looking to the Common. Some of the rooms were wainscoted in japan and a spacious gallery occupied the whole length of the house above and below stairs'.

Several houses were built on the estate: The Cedars in 1718, nos. 30-31 North Side in 1752 and The Elms in 1754. The last-named, of which a photograph is reproduced, stood in front of the site where the Hewer house had been, and was erected for a City stationer, Thomas Page, who died there in 1762. In 1783 Robert Barclay, a City banker, went to live at no. 31 nearby, and when the larger house became vacant in the following year he moved there. The next tenant of note was the architect Sir Charles Barry who came in 1853. He was born in 1795, the son of a Westminster stationer, and devoted his whole life to architecture. Country houses, clubs, churches and town halls up and down the country witness to his ability, but his greatest and best-known work was the rebuilding of the Houses of Parliament after the disastrous fire of 1834. Most of his work was completed by the time he came to Clapham and his large practice was in the hands of his sons, Charles and Edward Middleton Barry. While living at The Elms he bought and developed the adjoining estate and the two tall terraces (33-37 and 38-42 North Side), which flank the top of Victoria Rise; and the large mansions at the upper end of that road were probably designed in his office by E. M. Barry. Sir Charles died in his

36

36. The Elms, 29 North Side, Clapham Common

wife's arms at The Elms on 12 May 1860, and lies buried in the nave of Westminster Abbey. The house was bought in 1900 by the National Free Home for the Dying which in 1907 acquired no. 30, with the addition of no. 31 as a nurses' home in 1931. The last-named is interesting as having been the home (then known as The Hollies) of the architect J. T. Knowles (1831-1908), later the founder of *Nineteenth Century Magazine*. He designed a country house for Lord Tennyson at Aldworth, and the Poet Laureate several times visited him at Clapham. On one occasion Knowles gave a garden-party at which the main attraction was a little tent on the lawn with Tennyson and Browning ensconced within receiving favoured guests. After his removal to Westminster, Knowles became a friend of King Edward VII and was knighted by that monarch in 1903.

In 1917, the hospice became known as the Hostel of God; the present name dates from 1980 when the order that had run the institution for over 80 years, the Sisters of St Margaret, found they were not able to find sufficient younger members to carry on their work. Within the hospice is a charming Chapel of 1933 (now altered) by W. H. Randall Blacking and, at the rear, an extensive and well-maintained garden laid-out by John Medhurst to honour the eminent garden consultant, Lanning Roper.

THE WILDERNESS

The lithograph 'Villa of the late James Brogden Esq., MP' shows the front view of a fine mansion designed by the architect Henry Flitcroft (1697-1769) for Henry Hoare, a partner in the Fleet Street banking firm of that name. He had inherited the family seat at Stourhead in Wiltshire, and had there proceeded to lay out the magnificent gardens which now delight so many visitors. He was known as Henry the Magnificent, and in 1753, feeling the need for a house nearer to London, he built this villa on what had been part of the Hewer estate at Clapham. The main staircase mounted from a square hall to a first-floor gallery. Here were three

37. The Wilderness, Clapham, by Henry Flitcroft, 1753
38. The Cedars, North Side, Clapham Common, photograph by Henry Deane

reception rooms, the centre of which had a large bow-window looking out across the gardens to the river and to Chelsea beyond. When Henry Hoare died in 1785 he made over the Wiltshire estate to his grandson Henry Colt Hoare, the historian of Wiltshire, who had often stayed with him at Clapham; but the house there was sold and passed into the hands of John Brogden, a merchant in the Russia trade with a business in Leadenhall Street. The auctioneer described the house as 'an enviable retreat for a banker or merchant,

38

THE CEDARS

The photograph left was taken about 1850 by Clapham chemist Henry Deane, and shows the south front of a house which stood where Cedars Road was afterwards built. It was at the south-western corner of the Hewer estate and was erected for John Jackson, the favourite nephew and heir of Samuel Pepys, who had married Anne Edgeley, a cousin of William Hewer and one of the beneficiaries under his will. The Jacksons remained at The Cedars until about 1724 when it was tenanted by Sir John Barnard, Lord Mayor of London in 1737. He lived there for some years, after which the house became the residence for a short period of a city merchant, Godfrey Thornton, before eventually passing to the Misses Horne who were there until 1821, when Benjamin Brown bought the property. He took a great interest in local affairs, became a church trustee, a member of the local Society for Preventing Burglaries and a trustee of the parochial schools. At this period it became obvious that the schools needed larger premises and as there was no room for expansion in Old Town, Brown offered them a piece of land on the north side of the

environed by pleasure grounds and gardens laid out with great taste and judgement'. The front drawing-room had 'the walls exquisitely painted in subjects from the Mythology, by an Italian artist', and there was a large library on the ground floor. John Brogden died in 1800 and was buried in Narborough in Leicestershire, but his family continued to reside here for another 38 years. His eldest son, James, was a major in the cavalry company of the Armed Association. His daughter, Susan, married Thomas Astle, son of another Thomas Astle, the antiquary and Keeper of the Records who lived on Battersea Rise. The house was demolished in 1851, and Victoria Rise laid out.

Common. The offer was accepted and a boys' school was erected in 1838 which remained in use as a school until 1974. Benjamin Brown was a partner in a family business in Cheapside which failed in 1845, and as a result the Clapham home was sold. In 1860 The Cedars was demolished and the site developed. The architect of the new houses was J. T. Knowles.

The Cedars was a three-storey house of red brick with, at roof level, a platform with wrought-iron balustrade from which there was a splendid and wide-ranging view over the countryside. The garden front, known from a sketch by Joseph Powell, had a three-sided projecting bay and the main entrance on the west had a brick pediment above the central block. Several cedars of Lebanon stood on the lawn in front of the house.

39

39. North Side, Clapham Common with John Hatchard's house in centre
40. Portrait of John Hatchard, bookseller

JOHN HATCHARD

John Hatchard, the founder of the bookselling firm in Piccadilly, was born in 1768 in Castle Street, Westminster, and was educated at the Grey Coat Hospital. After a few years as an apprentice bookseller, Hatchard decided to begin a business on his own account, and this he did in 1797 with a capital of £5, taking a shop at 173 Piccadilly. He soon prospered,

40

and in 1801 took larger premises at 190 Piccadilly where the firm still remains, though there is no longer any family connection. His first publishing venture was a political pamphlet, *Reform or Ruin: take your Choice*, which was a phenomenal success. Hatchard's bookshop soon became one of the best known in town. Among his many distinguished customers he numbered Queen Charlotte, who bought numerous books on religious subjects and on history and natural history; William Wilberforce, who had letters addressed to him there; Pye, the poet laureate; the Macaulays, father and son; and Hannah More.

The Royal Horticultural Society in 1804 held its first full meeting 'at the house of Mr Hatchard', and in 1815 contributions to the 'Waterloo Subscriptions' for the orphans of those killed in that desperate battle were received at his shop.

Hatchard lived over the shop in Piccadilly for most of his life, and there six of his nine children were born. In 1821, however, when he was 53 years of age, he leased a pleasant modern villa on the north side of Clapham Common called Stonely House, which is the centre house in the photograph opposite, with a pediment and a mansard roof. Here he died in 1849 at the age of 80, leaving a fortune of nearly £100,000. He was recalled by one who knew him as 'in appearance the very acme of respectability. He was invariably dressed in black. His coat was of the style of a bishop's frock coat, waistcoat buttoning to the throat with an entirely plain front, knee breeches and gaiters'. He was a gracious and kindly man and an unobtrusive supporter of many charities. The portrait reproduced here is by an unknown artist and hangs in the bookshop in Piccadilly. The house on North Side was pulled down about 1900.

THE PAVEMENT

Henry Deane, who recorded this area so admirably in the years between 1850 and 1860, took the lower photograph. To the left is a small one-storey building, the engine-house of the Clapham Fire Brigade, a body that had a poor reputation for efficiency. Before the advent of the brigade, this building, or an earlier one on the same site, was the Cage or Lock-up, where thieves, drunks, or vagrants could be locked away for the night by the watchmen. Some building was on this site from at least the seventeenth century.

The gabled building, in the centre, occupied by a baker and a greengrocer, was very old, and was destroyed by a bomb during the last war.

The photograph on the right (taken by the Universal Photo. Co. of 25 The Pavement) is a very charming view of Victorian Clapham depicting The Pavement as it curves round towards The Plough. Brighton House and the pair of villas with the delicate ironwork verandahs have long since gone. Brighton House was so called because in 1827 the Brighton coach left from there twice daily, and seats could be booked in the shop.

Two more photographs by Henry Deane depict the scene further along

The Pavement. Figure 44 overpage shows from right to left nos. 23-6, all of which have long since had shop fronts built over their gardens. No. 26, in the years before the war of 1939-45, was a wonderful second-hand bookshop kept by Mr Henry Gallop, in which it was possible to purchase enough books to form a reasonably-sized library at prices ranging from a penny to two shillings.

41

41. Cock Tavern and the Old Fire Station, c.1860, photograph by Henry Deane
42. The Pavement, 1869
43. The Cock Tavern

THE COCK TAVERN

The Cock Tavern (now renamed 'The Frog and Forget-Me-Not') was one of the older Clapham public houses, although the earliest reference to it in the parish records is 1722. It was completely rebuilt in 1904, and altered again recently. In this photograph taken by Henry Deane about 1855 can be seen an amusing group of road menders posing outside for the benefit of the photographer. On the wall the street nameplate, The Pavement, is an old name which appears in a deed of the reign of King James I.

Next door, in 1869, was Edward Fox, photographer, who had a store of old photographs of large Clapham houses, long since destroyed, and nearly all of them, alas, untitled. Finally, the double-fronted shop of Batten and Davies, booksellers, printers and stationers: it had been a printers since 1773 and in 1827 belonged to H. N. Batten who had there a lending library of some 9,000 volumes and a reading-room where daily papers, reviews, and magazines could be read, and which was open from 9am to 9pm. The shop had small-paned windows and a pleasing balcony with iron trellis-work above. In the foreground is the Cock Pond, the deep end railed round for safety after a fatality at Christmas time in 1804 when it was frozen over. The gap in the railings was to allow access to the shallow part for watering horses.

The four-storeyed shop in figure 45 is that of Henry Deane himself. It had been a grocer's, Bull and Tewsley, when in 1824 it was rebuilt, and in 1837 it was taken by Deane as a chemist's. As no. 17 The Pavement it still stands, the finest shopfront in the locality, though it has long since lost its small-paned windows if not the decorative ironwork of its balcony. The next pair of shops are weather-

44

45

*44. The Pavement and the Cock Pond,
c.1860*

45. Deane's shop, 17 The Pavement

boarded at the back and may be
older than would appear from their
street frontage. Henry Deane lived
above the shop with his assistants,
who had a sword-stick with which to
arm themselves before answering the
nightbell, as the Common was infested
with footpads and undesirables after
dark. Though of Quaker stock, he
was married at Holy Trinity Church
in 1843, and as a result was expelled
from the Society of Friends. He
eventually became a churchwarden.
His bride was a Miss Jemima Elliott,

who had kept a girls' school in Old Town, at Weimar House. Deane is said to have been a kindly man, sympathetic to those of a younger generation and much esteemed by his professional colleagues. He was a familiar figure about Clapham with his bushy beard, long black overcoat, and a black canvas bag clutched always in his hand. He died quite suddenly on a visit to his son in Dover in 1874, and is buried in his wife's family grave in Cheriton churchyard. The trees on the right-hand side of the photograph are on the patch of green at the road junction still known as Clapham Cross.

THE PLOUGH INN

The Plough Inn, at the south-west end of the High Street at Clapham Cross, is first mentioned in 1729, but there had undoubtedly been an inn there for a longer period. In 1816 it was the scene of a disastrous fire which broke out in the taproom in the early hours of the morning of 29 May. The family and the few guests who were staying there managed to get out of the building in time and no lives were lost; but the inn was entirely destroyed, together with the elegant ballroom adjoining. It was not insured, and a public subscription was opened for the landlord and his wife. The premises were soon rebuilt, and apart from Victorian alterations to the façade, as seen in the photograph of 1926, it remained virtually unchanged until given its mock-Tudor front shortly after. The entrance to the yard, once used by coaches, then by Tilling's horse buses, and later as a horse-tram depot, was filled in and became a dining room. Adjoining on the right is the site of one of the early cinemas of Clapham: 'the Electric Palace Picture Playhouse. Refined, Amusing, Continuous Performance.' It opened in 1910. The entrance was round the corner in Venn Street, although the faience-

46

46. The Plough Inn, 1926

faced building shown was to have been the entrance to the Clapham Coliseum of 1919 (which in fact never opened as a cinema).

The elegant ballroom, lost when the inn was burnt down, is described in 1801 as 'a spacious and genteel assembly room where the gentry of the village and its environs hold their balls, assemblies, etc. Here is also an elegant coffee room facing the public road, where a great many of the London morning papers are taken in, which is frequented by gentleman of the first character and respect. Large companies are sometimes entertained with dinners, etc. at this house, the rooms being particularly well adapted for this purpose. Its custom is much improved by the civility and hospitality of the present possessor who is likewise careful to accommodate his customers with wines and other liquors of the first perfection. Behind the house is a spacious bowling green.'

GRAFTON SQUARE

Grafton Square was developed by Captain Thomas Ross, an Irish captain in the militia from Acton, Middlesex, who began to lay out the square in 1846. A nearby resident records that in the autumn of 1847 the glow of a vast fire in the Old Town reddened the sky of Clapham, and that it started in a workshop full of building material in what was then called 'Captain Ross's Square'. This perhaps was the end of the 'great house'. The fire may have delayed development, and the New Square was not completed until 1851. It remains very little altered with terraces of tall houses on two sides and rather smaller villas on the third, which can be seen in Deane's photograph. The fourth side was never built, but was eventually formed by the building of Offerton Road. In the centre of the square was a railed-in garden, with shrubs and lawns and flowers in large stone vases. The south-east corner site was left vacant, and many years later was taken for the new Baptist chapel. On the road entering the square from opposite the Polygon was built the new Congregational church, 1851-52, designed by John Tarring, a well-known architect of the period who specialised in Nonconformist places of worship, and whose splendid spire was an ornament and a landmark until it was damaged by a flying bomb in 1944 and pulled down ten years later. It forms the central feature of the photograph which seems to portray the quiet peacefulness of a Victorian Sunday afternoon.

Until about 1846 a large seventeenth-century mansion had stood there, belonging to the Daniel family who acquired the estate in 1641. Sir Peter Daniel, Sheriff of the City of London in 1683 and Member of Parliament for Southwark in 1685, rebuilt the house in 1690 and not long afterwards sold the Old Town frontage for building sites. When he died in 1700 his widow moved to a smaller house and let the 'great house' to another City merchant, who was a churchwarden at the time, William Lethieullier. The sole surviving male heir of the Daniels was Lionel, whose daughter Elizabeth married the 3rd Viscount of Torrington. His son's diaries of travels throughout England were published in 1934, and make very interesting reading, but they contain only a few rather patronising references to Clapham.

The Lethieulliers were a well-known Huguenot family, and William was a wealthy turkey merchant in London, and he, and his wife after him, lived in the Clapham house until 1741. They had numerous children, most of whom married into local families, but the second daughter, Sarah, married Thomas Loveday of Caversham, and an attractive series of family portraits remain in the possession of her descendants. They also have a sampler which she completed in August 1695 in her twelfth year bearing the lines 'Favour is deceitful and beauty is vain but a woman that feareth the Lord she shall be praised'. The next tenant was Sir John Barnard who remained until his death in 1764. The Thornton Astell family, who had made a fortune from the South Sea Bubble, bought the estate in 1785.

They moved away in 1812, and by then the old house had begun to lose its attraction.

47. *Grafton Square, c.1860, photograph by Henry Deane*
48. *The Thornton-Astell house at Clapham*

CLAPHAM FROM THE AIR

The three aerial photographs taken in 1930 on this and the following pages show in considerable detail most of the central part of the old parish of Clapham, and indeed provide in one or two cases the only record of certain buildings in the area.

Fig. 49 (right) has the church of Holy Trinity (1776) in the foreground, Nelson Terrace (c.1838) to the left and behind it the boys' school (1838). The five-sided block in the centre is the Polygon (1792) with the spire of the Congregational (now United Reform) church (1852) in Grafton Square behind it. In front of this is the row of eighteenth-century houses, the line of which is broken by the rebuilt 'Sun'. The tree-shaded gardens behind are now the site of Battley Brothers printing works. Next comes a long gabled building standing back from the road, which is Clapham Hall, of which no other picture is known. It was built in 1761 as a successor to an earlier Congregational chapel in Old Town near the school, and was in use as such until 1861 when it was bought by Mr Amon Winterbottom for use as a gymnasium. It was used for concerts and exhibitions for many years until, in 1904, it was converted into a factory and finally demolished in 1939 when Maritime House, the headquarters of the National Union of Seamen, was built on the site. Next door was a doctor's house (also demolished to make way for Maritime House) and, just beyond the turning leading to Grafton Square, a fire station (since rebuilt) on the site of Cedar House. Across the centre of the picture runs the line of The Pavement. Downer's Cottages are behind the Cock Tavern and the tall houses of The Sweep are partly obscured by a group of trees.

49. Clapham from the air, 1930

Figure 50 has one corner masked by the wing of the plane. Orlando Road, Macaulay Road, and The Chase cross the foreground. Between the last two lie Church Buildings facing the Common, with cottages and stabling among the trees behind. Behind these again is the vast Victorian rectory with its large gardens, in Macaulay Road, where fêtes were held and garden parties and where on Empire Day the children from the nearby parochial school went in procession carrying flags. Across the Common lies South Side with, from the right, Notre Dame School in its large garden, Crescent Lane and the curved line of the Crescent in Crescent Grove, with at the far end Grove House still standing. The twin spires of the Roman Catholic and the Wesleyan churches are clearly visible, and between them the vast roof of the tram depot.

50 & 51. Clapham from the air, 1930

51

Figure 51 concentrates on the Old Town. In the foreground the backs of the eighteenth-century houses facing the fire station and the nearby St Peter's Vicarage with a fine wrought-iron gate. Behind and to the left, with a light patch on the roof, are the workshops of W. Bainbridge Reynolds (1845-1935), craftsmen in wrought iron, whose splendid work is to be found in cathedrals and churches throughout England and the Commonwealth. Where the road forks is the old school, and triangular group of houses behind mark the old rectory site. Rectory Grove curves away left towards Larkhall Rise.

CLAPHAM COMMON

Clapham Common was a popular subject for artists in the mid-18th century. Edward Webb (1805-54) was a loal artist and the father of Sir Aston Webb, the architect.

YE OLDE WINDMILL

The Windmill Inn on the Common is first mentioned in local records of 1729, but an ale-house of some kind may well have existed earlier. A post-mill stood hereabouts from the days of King Charles I, and the inn presumably takes its name from it. It was a popular subject with artists in the last century, and a well-known picture by J. P. Herring, engraved in 1862 with the title *Return from the Derby, Clapham Common*, depicts many well-known figures on the road, with the inn in the background. It is an animated scene and one which, to some extent, was repeated annually for another 60 years until the advent of the fast car. At the time this photograph was taken, in the early years of the present century, Thomas Tilling Ltd were using the extensive stabling.

PLAN OF CLAPHAM COMMON

The small plan made by J. Edwards in 1811 shows the site of the inn clearly marked, with a signpost and an iron pump on the grass plot in

52

53

Clapham Common, 1846.

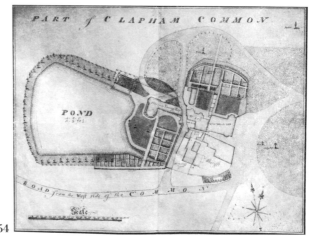

54

front of it. To the south was the stable block, and immediately behind was a house occupied by Mr Lett, with lawns and gardens. Beyond the narrow roadway was the larger house of Florance Young Esqr, the Southwark brewer to whose family the inn belonged. West of his estate was a large pond on the site of which is now a children's playground. In the 1840s Mr Lett's house was rented by Charles Pearson, a City solicitor who was active in the promotion of the Metropolitan Railway, but he unfortunately died just a few months before its opening. For him, one of the attractions of Clapham was that it was within easy distance of the City. 'Sixpence takes us by omnibus backwards and forwards,' he wrote.

His wife Mary was a portrait painter of distinction who exhibited for some 20 years at the Royal Academy.

55

The itinerant photographer on Clapham Common was caught in the act in 1877. The picture was originally printed in a scarce book, *Street Life in London*, by Adolphe Smith.

THE ROOKERY

A plan by J. Edwards, 1811, shows a group of cottages and stabling belonging to the Thornton family. John Thornton was a Russian merchant whose father came down from Hull in the early eighteenth century and built himself a house on the south side of the Common. The son, for a small annual payment, obtained permission from the Vestry to erect his stables on the Common on the opposite side of the main road. This unusual arrangement continued, seemingly without comment, until in about 1790 when his son Robert, who had a house next

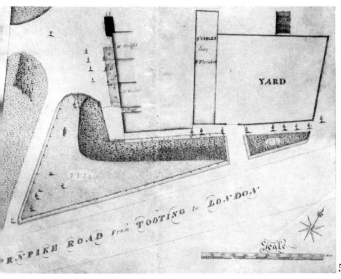

56

to his father, wished to erect additional building. Then there was considerable complaint from the parish. The buildings remained until the whole site was cleared in 1904, but they had long ceased to have any direct connection with the Thornton houses. They housed a veterinary surgeon, an ale-house, a washerwoman, and others. The undated pencil-sketch now in Guildhall Library shows the north-west corner of these buildings, by then known as The Rookery, facing onto the Common. Behind the bushes to the right was the Long Pond.

55. Photographer on Clapham Common in 1877
56. Plan by J. Edwards, 1811, part of Clapham Common
57. Pencil sketch of the Rookery, Clapham Common

57

SOUTH SIDE

South Side, Clapham Common, is part of one of the main roads out of London, the ancient Stane Street, but whether the Roman road followed the line of the present highway or carried on in a straight line from Clapham Rise, meeting the modern road again at Balham Hill, has not yet been proved. The little drawing below is a view of South Side by an amateur local artist, Alfred Webb, and is dated 1863. It shows the area now occupied by a group of buildings including the Alexandra Hotel, built in 1865. The tall house on the left is part of the newly built Cavendish Terrace where at no. 4, from 1864 to 1867, lived a young man named Julius Czarnikow

who had in 1854 come from north-east Germany to seek his fortune. He founded a business which still flourishes in the City, and when he died in 1909 he left assets worth over a million pounds. The terrace occupies the site of a house belonging to John Castell, a benefactor to local charities who has a memorial in Holy Trinity Church. Cavendish Terrace remains, but shops were built into the ground floors about 1900. Next come two small shops with bow-fronted windows occupied by Strachan and Burford (oil and colour warehouse).

58. South Side, Clapham Common, 1863

58

Two more cottages follow, the second having a shop built out in front and an ornamental iron balcony. It belonged to William Glaysher, white-smith and bell-hanger. Four more smaller cottages complete the row, the first and last being occupied by tradesmen with their signs outside. Grove's cottage was later used by Mr Sheldrick as an office for his coaches which ran daily to Blackfriars and Westminster. The third was, in April 1823, the scene of a terrible tragedy, a description of which takes up no less than 15 pages in a valuable little book published in 1827 by a local printer, H. N. Batten, entitled *A Key and Companion to the Plan of Clapham with its Common and Environs containing an historical and topographical description of the Parish and Manor with a Catalogue of Indigenous plants growing in the neighbourhood*. An elderly widow named Mrs Richards who had lived there for about 30 years was brutally murdered by a group of thieves who forced their way into the house. They escaped with what valuables they could find, but three of them were later brought to trial. One turned King's evidence and was pardoned; the other two were hanged.

On the right-hand edge of the picture appears the Baptist chapel built here in 1777. At that time it had a typical eighteenth-century frontage, a central doorway, two tiers of windows, the upper ones lighting a gallery, and in the pediment above an inscribed tablet. But in 1837 it was decided to modernise and improve the chapel by giving it more seating, and the gothic front which can be seen in the drawing. This did not please part of the congregation who considered that it smacked of popery, and one Clapham parishioner even complained to the rector about his permitting the erection of a Roman Catholic chapel. In due time the congregation needed yet larger premises, and in 1889 they moved to Grafton Square, while the building, with little alteration externally, became a post office. The post office was given a new and up-to-date neo-Georgian front in 1931 and then a few years ago it in its turn became too small and the frontage was again altered for a restaurant. But the gothic windows of 1837 remain in the side elevations and over a door reached by a side-passage is the tablet inscribed 'Baptist Meeting. Erected 1777'.

Deane's photograph is from much

59

the same viewpoint, but covers a wider area. To the left Cavendish Terrace is seen in entirety, followed by the curved frontage of Bellvue Terrace at the corner of Clapham Park Road, which is marked by the wooden signpost. Behind in the distance are the houses of High Street. The spire is that of the Roman Catholic church and dates from 1851, and the row of small houses to the right still stand although they too are now shops.

*59. South Side, Clapham Common, 1860, a calotype by Henry Deane
60. Plan of Clapham, 1827, published by H. N. Batten*

A PLAN
of
CLAPHAM
with the
Common
& its Environs.

The Walk by the Five Houses upon Battersea or Wandsworth Common, upon half Scale.

The Dwelling Houses are shaded thus
The Outhouses
The Public Houses are marked . . . P
The Mile stones are marked by a letter
A IV from Cornhill.
B III from Westminster Bridge.
C IV from London Bridge.
D IV from Blackfriars Bridge.
E V from Cornhill.
F 51 from Blackfriars Bridge.
51 from Westminster Bridge.
55 from London Bridge.
2 from Kennington Cross.
2 from Wandsworth.
83 from Kingston.
G is 1 mile distance from F.

CRESCENT GROVE

Gideon Mantell, medical practitioner and geologist, spent seven years of his life in Clapham, and the portrait of J. J. Masquerier was painted in 1837, the year before he arrived there. Having bought the practice of Sir W. Pearson, he moved into Crescent Lodge, South Side, on 29 September 1838. There has in the past been some discussion as to which house this actually was, due in the main to the fact that new owners frequently change the name of their houses. The drawing of 1840, here reproduced, is by George Scharf who illustrated some of Mantell's books, and there can be no doubt at all from this evidence that Crescent Lodge was the house to the left as you enter Crescent Grove.

61

SOUTH BUILDINGS

South Buildings, nos.32-4 South Side, has a tablet on no. 34 giving the date of their erection, 1812. The architect, J. T. Knowles, senior, lived at no. 2 South Buildings for a few years from 1840. No. 35, with projecting bay, is probably older.

Gideon Algernon Mantell was born in Lewes in 1790 and practised as a surgeon both there and later in Brighton. He soon made a name for himself as a geologist, particularly in connection with fossil remains discovered by him on the South Downs.

In Masquerier's portrait he is shown with a bone of the iguanodon, which he first identified in 1822. He sold his collection of fossils to the British

Museum before moving to Clapham, but he bought his other collections with him. He became one of the founders of a local scientific society, the Clapham Athenaeum, in 1841, and in the following year he was presented with a magnificent microscope by his friends in the locality 'in testimony of their grateful sense of his kind and effective exertions among them for the advancement of scientific knowledge'. The microscope was left by will to his son Reginald who later emigrated to New Zealand, and it is now in the Alexander Turnbull Library at Wellington. In contrast with the appreciation shown by his friends, he seems at this period to have had domestic difficulties, and his wife left him. In 1844 he moved to 19 Chester Square, returning each year to give his annual lecture to the Athenaeum. He died in 1852. He has been described as 'a man of abundant restless energy . . . fired with an ambition to become immortal in the realms of science'. Everything, even domestic happiness, appears to have been sacrificed to this ambition.

62

63

61. *South Building, built 1812*
62. *Dr. Mantell's house, Crescent Lodge, 1840*
63. *Portrait of Gideon Mantell, 1837*

64

THE ORANGERY, NOTRE DAME ESTATE

Large mansions began to appear along the south side of the Common in the eighteenth century, and among them was that of John Thornton, a pleasant house typical of its period with panelled rooms and ornamental plaster ceilings. It stood away to the right of our photograph (fig. 64), which shows a slightly larger house at one time occupied by his son Robert Thornton. In 1851 both were bought for a convent school run by a Belgian sisterhood, and the tall buildings which surround the old house were those built for the use of the school. In 1939 the sisters left and the estate became derelict. After the war the Notre Dame council housing estate, named after the school, was built on the site.

Robert Thornton (1757-1826) was the second son of John Thornton. Unlike most of the Thorntons, Robert had extravagant tastes, and was anxious to make his way in society. He enter-

65

tained lavishly, and in 1808 Queen Charlotte, with the Princesses Augusta and Elizabeth, honoured him with a visit. In the following year a similar entertainment was attended by the Duke of Gloucester and many of the nobility. It became obvious to his family that he was living beyond his means, and in 1810 the crash came.

66

67

In 1814 he fled to America to avoid his creditors, and never returned.

One of the principal ornaments of the garden was the beautiful Orangery, designed in 1793 by Dr William Burgh of York. The half-columns were of Portland stone, the capitals and ornamental work of Coade stone, and on the entablature was carved a quotation from Virgil's *Georgics*. Great glazed double-sashes kept the winter air from the plants, and could in summer be lifted when the Orangery was cleared and used to entertain guests. Within there was a marble tablet inscribed with 19 lines from *The Task* by William Cowper. Hereabouts, also, was a rockwork grotto.

JOHN THORNTON OF CLAPHAM

This portrait by Gainsborough of John Thornton hangs in the offices of

64. Notre Dame Convent School
65. The Orangery, Notre Dame Estate
66. Painting of John Thornton, by Gainsborough
67. Samuel Thornton, 1827, engraving by Charles Turner

the Marine Society of which he was treasurer from 1756 to 1783. John Thornton was born in 1720 and entered his father's business at an early age. He became a Member of Parliament, Governor of the Bank of England and of the Russia Company, and High Sheriff of Surrey. His typical John Bull figure is well portrayed in the painting. His eldest son, Samuel, took over the family business, was also a Member of Parliament, became a Director of the Bank of England and supporter of the Clapham Sect. He was born in Clapham and lived in a large house in Clapham Park Road.

68

JOHN ALLNUTT'S ESTATE

The area in which Elms Road now leads off South Side, Clapham Common was once the estate of John Allnutt, a prosperous wine merchant of Westminster. He bought it in 1802 from Samuel Smith, a city merchant who was great-grandfather to Florence Nightingale. The water-colour of 1852 by David Cox Junior shows the garden front of the house with the new greenhouse. This and the picture gallery (which is behind the greenhouse and not visible in the painting) were designed by J. B. Papworth in 1833. John Allnutt first married Elizabeth Garthwaite, who died young, and secondly, in 1811, Eleanora Brandram. All three were the subjects of splendid portraits by Thomas Lawrence, who was a friend of the family. By his second wife Allnutt had two daughters, one of whom, Jane, in 1845 married Henry Carr, an engineer. A painting of the wedding breakfast in the picture gallery, again by David Cox Junior, is the illustration, 69. John Allnutt died in 1863, when the estate was sold for development to a Mr Myers for £24,000. His remarkable collection of pictures was dispersed in a three-day sale at Christie's. Among the treasures of his library was the superb copy of Ackermann's *Westminster Abbey*, specially printed on vellum for the author. In 1925 it was presented to the Abbey by Queen Mary and is on exhibition there.

69

68. Water-colour of John Allnutt's house, 1852
69. The wedding breakfast of Jane Allnutt, 1845
70. The grounds of John Allnutt's house, 1853

The picture shows a view of the Gardens, painted in 1863 by H. Hopley White just before they vanished for ever. Flanking the entrance to the path are two tall vases filled with scarlet geraniums. William Keane in his *Beauties of Surrey*, 1849, has a long description of the estate, referring especially to the rustic-work verandah hung with wisteria (visible in the view of the house), the cedars of Lebanon, cypress and beech trees, the rose garden, the two green-houses, one full of camellia and azalia plants, the vineries, strawberry-pits and the rhododendron walk.

STOWEY HOUSE

The original Stowey House on South Side was built about 1730. From 1769 to 1775 it was occupied by Thomas Delaval, a member of the eccentric Northumberland family. In 1856 it became the Rectory, the parsonage in Old Town being too small to accommodate a rector with four sons and eight daughters; and it was then that the house was almost doubled in size, a new and taller building being added at the front, with stabling at one side. The Reverend W. H. W. Atkins Bowyer lived there until his death in 1872, and it was in this house that a terrible tragedy occurred. His little son was killed as a result of falling from the balustrade of the main staircase.

In 1873 the house was taken by Major-General Richard Strachey and his wife, recently returned from India, and it was they who named it Stowey after the village in Somerset where their family seat was situated. Four of their ten children were born in Clapham, the best known being the writer Giles Lytton Strachey, who was born there in 1880. At this time the house was a centre of Victorian literary and scientific society and included such visitors as Robert Browning, George Eliot, T. H. Huxley and G. F. Watts.

The Stracheys moved to Lancaster Gate in 1884 and the next occupants were the Urwicks, long established in the City as wine merchants.

William Urwick can be seen in the photograph seated on the balustrade with his daughter at his side. The house was demolished in 1966 to make way for an extension of the Henry Thornton school.

71

71. Stowey House, South Side

CLAPHAM LODGE

In *Peacock's Polite Repository and Pocket Companion*, 1822, is a tiny engraving, 'Villa of Spencer Meredith Esqr. Clapham Common'. Built only about two years previously, it lay well back from the road on South Side. In December 1835 John Wild, a wealthy City wine-merchant married and set up house at Clapham Lodge, as it became known. The house, now offices, still stands and warehouses have been built on its lovely lawns.

72. Villa of Spencer Meredith, later known as Clapham Lodge
73. John Wild of Clapham Common, 1848

CAVENDISH HOUSE

Cavendish House was another of the major eighteenth-century houses on South Side, though it did not bear this name in its earlier days. Its first owner was a banker named Henton Brown who, for a small annual payment, obtained permission from the parish to enclose the Mount Pond, which was on the Common almost opposite his house, and to erect a summer house on the mount so that he might entertain guests there. He also piped water from the pond across the road to his residence. In 1772 he evidently made some alterations, as old photographs show ornamental panels in the hall, signed 'Nollekens 1772'. In 1782 the bank which he had founded failed, and the estate was bought by Henry Cavendish, the scientist grandson of the second Duke of Devonshire. He turned the house into a vast laboratory and lived there the life of a recluse. It was here in 1798 that he carried out his notable experiment of weighing the world, and here that he died in 1810. Henry Cavendish never allowed his portrait to be painted, and the likeness by William Alexander was drawn by stealth at the Royal Society Club which Cavendish regularly attended. Sir Humphrey Davy, who knew him well, wrote that he 'was a great man, with extraordinary singularities. His voice was squeaking, his manner nervous, he was afraid of strangers and seemed when embarrassed to articulate with difficulty. He was enormously rich but made no use of his wealth.'

John Thornton, the son of Samuel Thornton, lived there for a few years before moving to The Terrace in the High Street; and Thomas Cubitt spent some time here too.

In 1833 William Herbert, another builder and developer, took his place, and it was he who greatly enlarged the house with a grand reception room, additional servants' wing and a terrace along the garden frontage. The two photographs taken some years later show this development. At some period the original red-brick central block had also been stuccoed over. Herbert died in 1863, and the house was taken by Henry Sanford Bicknell, who had married a daughter of David Roberts. R. A. Bicknell was a patron of many contemporary artists and had a very large collection in the house. On the death of his father-in-law he inherited a great many more excellent paintings and had to make a further addition to the

74

75

house in order to hang them. At the time of his death in 1880 the house was described by the auctioneers as 'a capital family residence with a suite of well-proportioned reception rooms, elegant drawing room, noble dining room, handsome library, morning room and billiard room, a large conservatory and 17 bed rooms.' The pleasure grounds were 'enriched with stately timber of oak, cedar, beech, fir and cypress, laid out with a terrace walk, lake and summerhouse' and beyond were the kitchen garden, greenhouse, orchid house, aloe-house and vineries. A most charming residence for a family of distinction.' It was bought by a Mr Hett who remained until 1899. In 1905 the estate was sold for building land, the house was demolished and the beautiful grounds vanished for ever beneath rows of red-brick villas.

74. Cavendish House, from Clapham Common, c.1880
75. Henry Cavendish, by William Alexander, in the old-fashioned garb which he always wore

76. West Side, Clapham Common, post- card c.1920

77

78

77. The Avenue, West Side,
Common Clapham

78. West Side, postcard c.1920

BATTERSEA RISE HOUSE

This imposing mansion was the home of Henry Thornton, the banker and leading member of the Clapham Sect, from 1792 until his death in 1815. For several years, as bachelors, he and William Wilberforce lived there together and the house became the unofficial headquarters of the Anti-Slavery Movement. Within was an oval library which opened onto the lawn.

The house was sold in 1907 and demolished shortly thereafter to make way for the housing along Canford and Muncaster Roads.

The view of West Side looking south shows, at the right, part of Western Lodge, a house built in about 1800. During the last century it was the home of several distinguished residents. In 1815 it was tenanted by Richard Thornton, who made a vast fortune by speculating in tallow on the Baltic Exchange. Sir James Mackintosh, lawyer and Whig historian lived there for a short period from 1828 as did, in 1843, Sir Charles Trevelyan who had married Hannah, sister of Thomas Babington Macaulay.

Adjoining is no. 83 West Side, which is believed to have been taken in 1868 by the famous opera star, Adelina Patti, one of several houses locally known to have been tenanted by her.

79. Battersea Rise House, West Side

80. West Side, postcard c.1920

80

THE HIGH STREET

The stores in this photograph of about 1890 stood in the High Street just on the London side of Wirtemberg Street. The business was founded in 1829 by a Mr Gibbs who was succeeded by E. J. Wright in 1848. Wright extended it and in 1886 sold out to Richard Grice and Son. It took in nos.106, 108, and 112 High Street, with cellarage beneath several other shops, but the business never managed to acquire no.110. Shortly before the First World War it closed down and the premises were demolished; the Majestic Theatre (architect: J. Stanley Beard) was built on the site in 1914.

In the old photograph reproduced here two houses (behind the Hosiers and Outfitters), now nos. 136-8 Clapham High Street, are of interest. Originally one house, they were from 1788 and 1835 the home of Captain Cook's widow Elizabeth and, for 20 years that of her cousin, Admiral Isaac Cook. As a boy he had accompanied Captain Cook on a voyage to the South Seas and according to family tradition was the first Englishman to set foot on the newly-discovered continent of Australia.

81

82

83

81. 'The Stores', Clapham High Street
82. Mrs. Cook's house, Clapham High Street, 1931
83. Mrs. Elizabeth Cook, portrait by W. Henderson, 1830

Elizabeth Cook was born in Wapping in 1741 and married at the parish church of St Margaret, Barking, in 1762. Her life seems to have been a sad one, for by the time she came to Clapham three of her sons and her only daughter were dead and her husband had been killed in Hawaii in 1779. Nevertheless, a friend wrote in 1792, 'She lives in high style at Clapham and keeps a footman'. She dressed always in black satin, and wore a ring containing a lock of her husband's hair.

When she died in 1825, a very old lady, she left £700 to the poor of Clapham, but was buried in St Andrew's Church in Cambridge, beside two of her sons.

84

SIR TIMOTHY WALDO

Sir Timothy Waldo (1704-1786) was a lawyer by profession, with a house in Aldermanbury in the City. He was also a liveryman of the Salters' Company, and became Under-Sheriff in 1739. He prospered, and in 1750 deciding that he needed a country residence nearer than Hever Castle which he had bought five years earlier, he acquired a house on South Side, Clapham Common, near the Windmill

85

84. *Sir Timothy Waldo's house, Clapham High Street, 1780*
85. *Painting of Sir Timothy Waldo, by A. Ramsey*

Inn. He had married in 1736, and had one daughter, Jane, and in 1769 he was knighted. In 1776 he moved to a more splendid mansion in the High Street. It was a large house, shielded from the road by fir-trees and a tall fence, with an impressive pair of entrance gates opening on to a drive which led round past extensive stabling to the entrance door. At the rear of the house was a two-storey semi-circular bay, on the top of which a grand view could be obtained of Westminster and the City. In the meantime, his daughter Jane had married George Medley of Buxted in Sussex, and Sir Timothy died there while on a visit and was buried in the churchyard. His widow 'who lived and died an example of every Christian virtue', died in 1806, and his daughter Jane in 1832. The Clapham property then reverted to another Jane Waldo, a cousin, who lived there until 1840. After some years as a school, the house was demolished in 1880, and shops and a tram depot occupied the site. The portrait of Sir Timothy Waldo was painted by A. Ramsay about 1750, and shows him resplendent in a grey-green coat and blue waistcoat, heavily embroidered in gold.

86

87

PRESCOTT PLACE

Prescott Place was a street of small cottages lying between Wirtemberg and Manor Street, and with Cross Street, Chip Street and Manor Lane (Little Manor Street), was built about 1820-30. It probably took its name from a family of Colonel Prescott who was in command of the Armed Association from 1803 to 1812 when he was presented with a sword in recognition of his valuable services. His house is next to the former Majestic Cinema in the High Street. Prescott Place was a continuation of Manor Lane which led up beside the Two Brewers public house. In earlier days this was a typical country tavern lying back from the road, with a horse-trough in front of it and a sign swinging from a lofty pole.

BICKLEY PLACE

The Clapham Rectory Estate, a warren of small courts and alleyways just north of the High Street, was swept away at the close of the last century when Venn Street was built and Bromell's Road re-aligned. Bromell's Buildings led out of Bromell's Road towards Wirtemberg Street, with Waterloo Place leading to Waterloo

Retreat, Cooper's Cottages and Hook's Cottages, and Hume Place just past the Beehive public house. Waterloo Place appears again in figure 88, with Bickley Place, figure 87, which led out of the north side of Bromell's Road next to Bolton Court, the site being now covered by Venn Street. Vine Cottages vanished, unrecorded.

86. *Prescott Place, 1956*
87. *Bickley Place*
88. *Waterloo Place*

88

89

90

THE BOWYER ARMS

The Bowyer Arms, Manor Street, was built by Thomas Cubitt in 1846, and in the accompanying photograph of 1909 can be seen the family arms as used by William Atkins Bowyer who died in 1844. The same coat, said to have come from the Manor House when it was demolished, appears above a shopfront in Old Town. The arms on the public house was unfortunately destroyed many years ago, but a modern painting of the Bowyer family arms was erected as an inn sign in 1968. In what was once a basement kitchen, an old bread-oven is preserved, and in a large room upstairs the Bowyer Musical Society used to meet.

Manor Street is one of the most pleasant early Victorian streets in

89. Waterloo Place, 1896
90. Bromells Buildings looking towards Wirtemberg Street
91. The Bowyer arms, Manor Street, in 1900

91

Clapham. A large building just beyond the Bowyer Arms was designed by J. T. Knowles for the Clapham General Dispensary, established in 1849. One or two of the earlier residents are perhaps worthy of brief mention. At no. 40 lived for many years Tobias Matthay, a distinguished music teacher, composer, and author. Born nearby at no. 1 Turret Place in 1858, he lived in Clapham until he married in 1893. In 1906 the Tobias Matthay Pianoforte School opened in Oxford Street. At no. 34 lived Edwin Mayall, photographer, eldest son and one-time partner of the better-known J. J. E. Mayall of Regent Street. At no. 10 lived W. R. Cory with his family, and on their grave in West Norwood Cemetry it is recorded that his eldest son, William Henry, rode as 'one of the 600 in the Charge of the Light Brigade at Balaclava Oct 25th 1854'. He survived and died years later in America.

THURSTON HOUSE

92

Thurston House, an eighteenth-century house in Rectory Grove, was named after a former owner. The photographs show adornments to the entrance doorway and to the arch of what was probably once a stable block made of Coade stone. This was an artificial stone made by a secret process by Mrs Eleanor Coade whose business was on a site now covered by County Hall, close to Westminster Bridge and in the London Borough of Lambeth.

The house has recently been completely and sensitively refurbished and provides accommodation for people recovering from the effects of alcohol or drug dependancy.

93

92. Thurston House, Rectory Grove
93. Coade-stone keystone, Thurston House
94. Entrance to Thurston House, Rectory Grove

94

CLAPHAM PARK

ATKINS ROAD

Clapham Park was laid out as a residential area by Thomas Cubitt, who in 1825 bought up 229 acres of the Bleak Hall Farm estate, together with a mansion house and ground. New roads were cut, and plots marked out, but purchasers did not appear as rapidly as the builder had hoped, and the venture was not an unqualified success; nevertheless in the mid-nineteenth century Clapham Park was undoubtedly one of the most important of London suburban districts. Atkins Road, one of the first to be formed, was named after William Atkins, Lord of the Manor, and a modest-sized house was built

95

96

95. 39 Atkins Road, Clapham Park, 1949
96. 138 New Park Road, water-colour, undated

there for the Clerk of the Works. Other more imposing residences followed, and residents have included Sir John Bennett, whose famous clock was once one of the City sights in Cheapside, Jack Hobbs (Sir John Berry Hobbs) the cricketer, Dan Leno, and Adelina Patti, the world-famous operatic singer. Precisely where she lived remains a mystery. Pierrepoint House was said to have been the name of her residence in the summer seasons of 1863-8, but no house of that name can be identified. Jack Hobbs lived for some years from 1928 at no. 39, mentioned above as the first house to be built and shown in the photograph, taken in 1949, below. It was pulled down soon afterwards. In his earlier years he was sometimes to be seen playing cricket on Clapham Common.

NEW PARK ROAD

The water-colour above is from the Guildhall Library, and is an early view of another villa on the fringe of Clapham Park. It depicts the present 138 New Park Road, not long after it was built in 1835, when the district was still semi-rural. Its first occupant was a retired broker named William Eicke, who lived there until his death in 1878. There is a strong tradition that the composer Verdi lived in this house on one of his visits to London. It is recorded that he was in London in 1847, 1862, and 1876, but we do not know where he stayed. Was William Eicke his host? There is no mention of him in any published work on Verdi.

New Park Road was also the home of two water-colour artists whose work is of considerable charm and ability: David Cox Junior, who lived at no. 82 from 1860 to 1876, and William Bennett who lived nearby at Bleak Hill Villa, and later at Milford Lodge from 1850 until his death in 1871. Both have memorials in Lambeth's West Norwood Cemetery, but their houses have gone, seemingly unrecorded.

KING'S AVENUE

No. 84 King's Avenue is one of the few remaining examples of Thomas Cubitt's development in Clapham Park. It is now turned into flats, and there are additions at the back. It was originally built in 1849: a large double-fronted house with enclosed porch and gas lamps beside the steps. Sir William Napier was the first occupant, naming it Scinde House after the Indian province conquered by his brother Charles in 1843. Born in Ireland in 1785, he entered the army at an early age and fought in the Peninsula campaign under Moore and Wellington. Wounded severely in 1809 by a bullet lodged in his spine, the removal of which was found to be impossible, he suffered considerable pain for the rest of his life. He retired to Clapham following his appointment as Governor of Guernsey (1842-48). He will be best remembered for his six-volume *History of the War in the Peninsula*, the abridgement *English Battles and Sieges in the Peninsula*, and for his book on the conquest of Scinde written in defence of his brother. He was a man of ardent, enthusiastic, and impetuous temperament, and an insatiable controversialist, writing innumerable letters to *The Times* and also, as his memorial at West Norwood Cemetery so justly says, 'he was the friend of the soldier and of the poor'. He died in 1860 and his widow survived him only six weeks.

This house passed into the hands of a distinguished lawyer named McNaughton, who changed the name to Dunderave after the family seat in Argyllshire. Early in the present century the house was renamed Victoria House after the music hall artiste Vesta Victoria who lived there for ten years. The name is still retained.

97

99

98

97. *Sir William Napier*
98. *84 King's Avenue, Clapham Park in 1949*
99. *Bedford Buildings, Clapham Park Road, built 1822*

BEDFORD BUILDINGS

'Bedford Buildings 1822' is carved on a tablet on no. 196 Clapham Park Road which, with its neighbour no. 194, comprises an interesting pair of late Georgian houses on the corner of King's Avenue. Their frontage was somewhat spoiled after the war by curtailment of the front garden, and they were just saved from un-authorised demolition in 1974. Sub-sequently, they have been converted by Lambeth Council into flats. In a directory of 1841 no. 196 was the res-idence of the Reverend William Foster, and no. 194 was a Seminary for Young Ladies kept by a Miss Catherine Foster.

CLAPHAM AT WAR

During the Second World War parts of Clapham Common were taken over for defence and other purposes. Public air raid shelters were constructed on North Side and elsewhere. Several deep shelters, each with a capacity for 4,000 persons, were constructed in the Clapham area, adjacent to each local Underground station. Below the running tunnels for the tube are pairs of large diameter tunnels, 1,400 ft. long.

Their sinister-looking ventilation shafts can still be seen.

Anti-aircraft gun batteries were placed on the Common and for one period they were commanded by Sir Mortimer Wheeler, the distinguished archaeologist.

Emergency pre-fabricated housing was erected by Long Road and remained until the mid-1950s.

100

101

102

103

100. Air-raid shelters under construction on the Common, 1939
101. Anti-aircraft battery, Clapham Common

102. 'Pill-box' or strong point of 1940 on Clapham Common
103. 'Prefab' housing, Long Road, Clapham Common

CLAPHAM COMMON. — NORTH SIDE.

North Side looking east towards Battersea Rise. In the distance is the tower of St Barnabas, 1898, (architect W. Bassett Smith), built on the front lawn of The Shrubbery, which still stands (in Lavender Gardens).

We are grateful to the following for illustrations. The Late Gordon Barnes, Battersea Library, London Borough of Wandsworth, Bernard Battley, British Museum, Clapham Antiquarian Society, Greater London Council, Ron Elam English Heritage, London Division, Guildhall Library, Corporation of London, Hatchards, Imperial War Museum, The Marine Society, Minet Library, London Borough of Lambeth, Nicholas Long, Raymond Ninnis, National Monuments Record, Frank Phillips, Royal Institute of British Architects, *The Times*, Wimbledon Library, London Borough of Merton, Wandsworth Central Library, London Borough of Wandsworth